Montreal on October

by

Ryan
Marcel
Buynak

I0172548

Montreal on October
All content Copyright © 2013 by Ryan Buynak

ISBN 9780985316877

All rights reserved.

Published by **The Paradisiac Group**
(Davenport, Iowa/Los Angeles, California/New York, New York)
www.theparadisiacgroup.com

No part of this book may be reproduced without
expressed written permission of the author or the publisher,
except for brief quotes for review purposes.

Coyote Blood, Inc.

Author Contact:
www.ryanbuynak.com
www.coyoteblood.blogspot.com
www.facebook.com/theryanbuynak

the amazing cover
of this book was designed by
Esther L. Kim
www.estherlkim.com

Other Silly Titles by Ryan Buynak

Enjoy the Regrets

Yo Quiero Mas Sangre: Random Acts of Poetry

The Ghost of the Wooden Squid: Random Acts of Poetry

"Surely there stand few nobler cities than Montreal –
surely none more fairly situated. Upon the banks of the
St. Lawrence, Montreal lifts her thousand roofs towards
the faint blue of the Canadian sky, and her sons speak
with many tongues of the young nation, to whose
enterprise and daring is a living, growing testament."

--Montreal by Gaslight,
1889, Anonymous

Freelance Florist

you can find me at Marche Atwater
on a given Thursday.
that's when the pretty vendors
get good new fine gone flowers.

pick up twenty to thirty different bouquets
and a bunch of lavender;
that's my signature,
and it smells so damn good.

picnic near the canal and create.
spread out a sheet and eat lunch,
then open up the bundles
and make my own big bastard saintly bouquets.

it all depends upon season and mood
and rain and what not;
some are small affairs with yellow spray roses,
some are big deals with sunflowers and tulips.

then I take my creations,
and sell them downtown
all weekend long to touchy tourists
for a good fine gone profit.

Park Ranger

Royal in my ways
of the path
that leads me to you
and here,
this place...
we call it Royal.

It seems too real
to a kid that I once knew.

He was hopeless,
from trailer parks.

He was...

Me.

Confidence is a Killer

There is a Rumbler in Montreal
and it takes me to and fro.
And it is nicer and cleaner than that of NYC.

While my brain burns slow,
deadlines make me shake,
just like the letter S.

Then straighten out,
like the letter K.

Pass the salt.
Pour the wine.
I am alright.
If you are alright.

Burp!

I burp with the best of them.
And I only fart in alleyways
and on airplanes.
Sorry, love.
You are trapped no matter what.

Silly

justify my ghost
in this hotel,
and be mine forever
without wandering
or wondering
what if.

just sing.

Give or Take

This Book is About 129 Pages.
Maybe burning at 130.
Maybe cooling at 132.

Will he ever knife it up to you?
And quietly understand?

Of a mountain,
I swallow the side
of a lightning strike,
in the valley where lovers lie.

Dead hearts
are
everywhere.

Get Sick, Get Better, Get Weird

Unless I had a Sunday,
there's a goat at the top of a clock,
and we are all old cucumbers.

Goons gone for rivers running
into deep blue cardinal suns,
your pillow is covered in mustard,
while mine is covered in burning
beverage napkins.

Hey there, little happy Squid,
who created the comma?

Some asshole.

I have a cowboy's eyes,
and I like your point of view.
We roam.
I fly.

Let loose the soft horizon,
it was a good thing
that I was your neck.

Let the crickets sing
until they die good deaths.

A glass of courtesy ketchup
for the killer cats with cancer in the alley,
and an autoharp given for my heart,
and doldrums for you and yours.

Can't kick the can
with your eyes closed.

One day as a lion.
One year as a liar.

In both myth and mornings,
this is the cannon duke,
like we drew with charcoal
before the dark.

Rue Sainte-Catherine

Oh, Sainte-Catherine! you will remember me forever.
You found us in the best of our weeping.
Nobody takes my mind off of you.
Oh, Sainte-Catherine! how you run up the stubborn.
You are a dark souvenir.

I watch you and your turrets
from the bastion no longer,
because I walked all over you.
I am not the man you desired.
Oh, Sainte-Catherine! I give you my heart and my shoes.

Oh, Sainte-Catherine! every morning and every evening.
It is so good to see you back here again.
Every year.
Just me and my lover,
and my marvelous regrets.
Not minding your movies or ever crossing you.

Use Me For Warmth

if you choose to go,
please be careful.

love will take your photograph.
if you frequent the same tooth-laced restaurant.

There is always a good song to listen to loud.

and I hope your life
gets tangled and knotted
in mine, again and again.

forget my yawns.
I am weak every week,
therefor never full,
forget about forgetting me.

This is what we work for.
Me and you.
And memories.

A Goddamn Good Kisser

I see your keys,
and I give us time.

glad to dig life,
glad to go write!
Tonight!

my heartbeats beat out of pace.

I know it is right,
and I am dumb,
but we should do it again.

Maybe. Forever.

While songs start,
and nights end.

this is our outer space.

Darn Farm

(for Kayle, for inspiring the title)

Wednesday's tomorrow,
the wicked,
and I,
the phone number
only.

platinum,
take your time,
hold on to my hand,
inside of forever,
forever being me,
and word forts.

Are you coming with us?
this buzz is this biz,
by the door and/or the window,
by the time,
by the tidal waves.

You've seen it all.
And I just want to thank Hashem for creating your eyes.
And mine.

Manage

I have never
lost my sky.

That which mentored
the ground
beneath my feet.

Just An Idea

I can't stop the buildings
from singing.
La la la la la la la.
Frisky.
Hey!
It's been eight years and it does not end.
I've lost my mind
a baker's dozen
times.

Fireworks and Figure Eights

Right in the Mile End.
Minute of it all.
Middle.
The ghost of your toes.
A better Brooklyn.
Similar to Portland.
But better than that, too.

Love that hand.
Bird art.
Tooth brush and a comb.
And that ring.
Gold.
On your finger.
And the pepper in the background.
Nest.

The wind blows cool and soft
into the second floor
of the restaurant
and my hands are reversed.

Maybe Rain

Maybe
I am
dreaming,
but
I can't sleep.

The house
and the horns
are the roof
and the shrine.

This ship will kill ya.

Where The Porters Weep

The sun is seen.
Sad through pianos.
Through scenes.
Screened through heaven.
And we forget the Devil.
While he rides away.
Outlaws always sail away.

Clap laps.
And crotches.
Harmonicas burn.
Bright.
The thought of someone being someone.

Wives.
Live.
While.
Other Loves.
Die.

Back to Penn Station.
Tonight.
Oh lord.
8 o'clock.

Wait.
For me.
Hold.
On.
Tight.

We grow.
We dance desperate to the sky's sun.

The Mailbox is Full

your life is in there,
cold like today,
with yellow leaves
and heavy breaths,
and hardened calves
from walking uphill.

the yellow lights mean nothing
to me,
I keep going...

Up.

Love Your Folk Heroes More Than Poems

Through the valley
where lovers climb,
and where the sunlight ends early,
and ends the day,
and follows the rain
with indecision.

I am an eager man.
I will never understand.

The Sobriquet

A whiskey in the window,
as cold in a nice night
and a Ray Ray raining daydream
as anything to ever come along in my little life.

That was last night,
but it was right, when I was a child
this is what I dreamed of:

A wife and a nickname.

Travel.

Guns.

Land.

Seasons.

A city.

Peacocks.

This morning my dream came true;
it was coffee
in a wide window on Rue Centre.
The bright, bright sun was a bonus.

And now,
I sit still in gardens
under graffiti, along Lachine Canal.

I gave up headphones
for the fine gone soundtrack
of this ville,
near Marche Atwater,
nearest to my wayward heart.

Iron Axe

I was saved by the fire,
and a knife,
and the sad sad sad folk song.

Keep my teeth, stupid fools.
Dead but dead.

no longer.
Paint my pinky nail.
The color of soulmates.

the same color as my pick-up truck.
where we blinked and fell in love.

Fall Here

this is my motherfucking meditation,
a painless destination.
Heartbeats and sex.
New wave leaves on the sidewalks
and I like feeling small.
I don't speak French but I don't give a shit,
just look at my tattoos.
The Earth is humble towards me in some places.
No sides, Aristotle.
The future is open.

The History of Electricity in Quebec

I unfold in the arms of the century,
and she is sterling and capitol.

Kurt Cobain was at my wedding.

An owl citizen,
I threw away some of my bad habits,
and all of my cocaine.

I pull on some dirty, olive-colored
jeans and an old t-shirt,
and I email my editor
to she if she has sent the royalty check
that I so deserve.

I started a novel,
here in Montreal,
two years ago and it is brilliant and finished,
but it is so good that I am
afraid to sell it.

It's like sending my child to her first day of school.

Then I catch myself
and try to laugh it off.
When I was twenty-four years old,
I tried to imagine this river
with no rules.

there is always a reconnoitering
before the battle.
strangle a could.
Or a would.
this is life, this is now, this is fun.
this is just the beginning.
this is how you make a time machine.

the commodore,
cap-locked to the fire in eyes of quick men,
hard working with rewards,
just like chaotic growth,
a significant role in the economic and political life of me.
let me put my notes away,
and start the day.
we will curl back around
to the sound,
where we laugh
and learn
to live again.

I unfold in the arms of the century,
and she is sterling.

And I am a lucky sonofabitch.

A Midnight Jam in Parc La Fontaine

streetwear in Montreal depicts a flannel overshirt every day.
I can play that part with one broken heart.
the folk musicians here all like me and give me couches.
and food and high-fives and drugs.
and let me borrow a skateboard for a couple heelflips.
I wish Vernon were here,
he'd get a kick out of these fine gone characters.
somehow, through the days I don't give in.
Satisfied with one Anglophone gig or two.
I believe these stories save the truth.
from a horrible death.
satisfied with sirens and one window and a tiger.
my cellular telephone is in a Chicago banquet room.
my violence is in Manhattan.
my time here is spent listening.
and longing to be someone new to someone new.
most nights, I dream of circles and graveyards.
One hundred dreams without numbers.
Satisfied, I am back to remaining.
if no one sees me, I am not here at all.
I carved some initials in the bark of a tree.
as proof of something called existence.
and then I petted a dog and left.

Poem

do you.
believe.
That.
there are still.
treasures.
in this ocean?

did I say.
That.
I am just.
a boy?

are we.
at the end.
of the world?

if not.
do you.
know how long.
it takes.
to get there?

do you feel pain?
uneven with soldier's eyes?

are those.
your only star-studded shoulders.
with which to cart this burden?

Mix CD, 1019

1. *Big Bird in a Small Cage* by **Patrick Watson**
2. *Don't Haunt This Place* by **The Rural Alberta Advantage**
3. *Toes* by **Lights**
4. *Karen Silkwood* by **Boxer the Horse**
5. *Souffle d'Ange* by **Le Vent du Nord**
6. *Run Mountain* by **The New Lost City Ramblers**
7. *Mexico City Subway Song* by **Matt Lipscombe**
8. *The Very Thought of You* by **Billie Holliday**
9. *Muse Blues* by **Loudon Wainright III**
10. *5* by **Breathe Owl Breathe**
11. *The Lime Tree* by **Trevor Hall**
12. *Yaa I Get It* by **Shad**
13. *Saintly Rows* by **Dear and The Headlights**
14. *The End* by **Kings of Leon**

Elevated

better than ever...

but
then again,
there are certain
things I should
never see or read again...

there are, however, things in which I certainly believe.

we won't go into those.

for the first time
in my entire uncertain life
I feel like an adult,
a real adult,
as I take off
my wrist watch
and put it on the
night's nightstand next to the
hotel bed,
I think these thoughts instead.

again,
it is raining tonight in Montreal.

my toes are terrible in airports and train stations.
my cellphone is dead and I am dying.

even with curses
these days,
these marbled, beautiful days
are better than before.

they are...
the human lawn.
a target in the sky.

Weapons

Sometimes.
All you need are fourteen songs.
Or a few shitty books of poetry.
Mostly about death.
But mostly about love.
to change the goddamn fucking world.

Elevated (Again)

the scales skin on hands,
drunk,
dragging on cigs,
and butter sticks
with devils' tears,
and it is time to shut up,
and that broken law
feels so good to
the gone.

photographs are both
proof,
and thieves.

I walk with a limp and a beer.
I heard the Wallflowers on the radio twice today.

it is still raining in Montreal.

money can't afford these dreams,
so good
as windows of late
and roses on certain
yellow-treed streets.

goodbye to those songs
and the radio
and the life
left below the elevated somewheres,
and the buried nowhere.

plans to be obsolete.
the eternal love.

I am somewhere, too.
I am happy there.

I am currently on Rue Sherbrooke and Saint-Urbain.
I am better off here.

happiness is relative...

I eat pizza and walk around.
I sing songs about the winter.
I never wonder where I am.
I gave up the telephone.
I don't care anymore.

be my lover, my lady river.

be my one life, my Saint of nowhere rivers and downed telephone
poles.

you are a beautiful town.

you are page thirty-two.
you are now forever.

Might Bribe The Year Just to Hear Me

I fix curses in grace,
and kill centipedes with love,
while trucks stop for kills,
and Montreal has my heated heart,
which I mailed from Florida via New York.

The sun eats itself,
and I eat the surrounding angry clouds
for Brunch.
I cannot catch up to life,
but I can slow it down
with riddles.

Then I pause,
and perceive the day down the alley,
and wish for a million wishes,
the first of which I would use
to freeze this moment forever,
the moment you came down the stairs
looking like an angel
designed just for me.

And I thank the sky
and whoever created it
for living above this day
like a taxed totem
giving us light
for this perfect candied day.

Poem, This Is It

that house in the forest
that forest in the middle
that middle in life
that life we call days
those days we call life.

somebody can see.
us.

Wonder Home Wander

come hang out.
I'm hungover.

I wasn't in this kitchen in 2001.
and I know I talk too much.

light me up another
and read my own poetry
out loud
to me
in our
beautiful bed.

it's a fire.
it's about you.

an hour in this life
with coffee and cigarettes,
and I am going to be good at this.

I felt fall coming since last spring.

I am a lost creek
that leads somewhere.

wandering and wondering
why sometimes Sundays
decide to sleep.

not gonna die with that ego.
never bored.
worth everything.
worth resurfacing.

kingsofar

I am not well
from wishing
over draw bridges
at 11:11pm.

on the goddamn LIRR.
Lindenhurst no more.
Love no less.

on the goddamn Amtrak
going north with the Hudson on the left
and the giant mythological Lake Champlain
come home on the right, in the red.

no one reads this shit anyway.
my prim poetry, pronounced so oddly,
with a weird accent, she'd say,
a mix of Florida and somewhere else.

this is a different train.
and a different train of thought.
This is north.
wobbling, let's call it The Wobbler.
this is all that I have.
plus the fresh air in my lungs,
the lint and the lighter in my pocket,
and the coins in my hand.

what a buzz to be me.
I think mirrors are funny friends,
like television sets
and other living rooms.

I wish I had the guts to scream.
Things are exactly what they seem.
Not *not* party to a mess,
Neverknowing can kill you.

Broken English

I've been dancing with your ghost
along this bronze river,
since the beginning bend,
trying to find strong drink
and adapt to the walls,
or else they will adapt to us.

This is what we trade our hearing for.

Someone's mouth starts to move,
giving us only broken English,
too much change,
and the heart of a hotel.

It's up to you to forget yourself,
and we will defiantly dance together forever,
until everybody and the earth moves,
or shakes,
or stands completely still.

The Thank-You Farm

walking down the east,
I suddenly miss my Harlem Farm,
but I don't miss White Harlem,
or that year,
or harvesting beer.

brothers in arms,
always,
they know why I carry a tomahawk;
they help me chop up a January
and burn an April.

We Are Somewhere Sending a Postcard to the Mountains

in the tired thick thistle,
in the doubt of the city,
do I have a night owl
or at the very least a carrier pigeon?

hold my hand
as we run from bandits
with saxophones instead of rifles.

let us detail the turn-away
and don't let birthday water
fall on a Friday.

the bandit came in, and just wanted to watch.

Toes

cross the street
and cross my heart
and hope to die
on your tippy toes.

A Typical Side Street in The Plateau

Half-curved yellow staircases.
Some are orange and some are green.
Just like the leaves of chronic autumn.
A churchbell tolls, probably on L'Avenue du Mont-Royal.

This neighborhood
believes in books
and smells so good
and each right or left
looks like a photograph.

Michel Tramblay and Mordechai Richler
used to walk these streets and write
under the dirt lights.
Leonard Cohen is probably at Bagel Etc.

These poems are tales for belated drinkers;
I am honored that I exist
inside these days;
I can still hear the *Joual* dialect.

myDreamcometruegirl

I know I am a goner.
Tomorrow is at my door.
But tomorrow ain't sure.

Today is beautiful.
And *She* is looking right through me.
with those sad beautiful eyes as sunflowers.

Every Girl Has Rules to Bend

In an automatic battle at the cinema
eventually you will be my mountain too.
Not like you but not like them.
The wind blows no matter where you are.

We are from an island just called *The.*
we invade your inlet
while riding on a red shooting star.
Fast bad news can't catch up with us.

I live and love here,
among broken feet and coolly rulers.
I listen here
for hearts and tongues, being burned by boys and soup.

Use the fabric
I keep
my memories sewn to...
City halls are rough canvases for the moon to paint.

Ghost Rain

I can hear the rain.
Its arrival.
Yet, I just cannot seem to see it.
Have my eyes turned into antlers?
My heart still ticks.
My legs still work.
I can still feel her sharp hips.
And the stars upon her shoulders.
And the peacock on her back.
But I cannot see the rain.
Even in puddles
Even on windshields of Honda Civics.
I feel the skywater.
Collecting in my mustache.
For I do not believe in umbrellas.
But I cannot taste it.

The Moon is in the Room

Sometimes,
the moon
retires
to a hotel room
in Montreal.

Every year,
the moon forgets itself,
and shakes off the sea of tranquility.

Room 304.

Did the moon
remember what it tried
to forget?
Nah, nah, nigga!
The moon forgot what it tried
to remember.

Poem

I crack my back
in the hallway
of an abandoned school,
and laugh
about hallways
in general.

Go reach your point
of view,
when and while
we find a way.

Annabell,
I have heartburn,
or a burning heart.

Where does the spirit go
when we die?

Love Notes and Other Stupid Soliloquies

One day I will die
but these days will be legacies,
and this goddamn poem
will be something, something.

The audience,
the fuckers who read this shit will love the honesty.

I write this in a hotel room in Montreal.
Same as the last one
and the first one.

I am just living,
eating room service pasta,
and looking at Instagram
and writing shitty poetry about love.
I am sorry, Audience.

The Jacques Cartier Bridge

Jacques Cartier was a French explorer,
and now he is a bridge,
on which I shift easy equipage.
The French music on the old radio
is the company of confused dreams.
A sonnet forms in my head
and I yell it out the window
at the rushing river down below.

Something My Soul Needs

I am unclean.
but I still worry more about you.
than you do about me.
I have no point.
Besides these written words.
My body is feeling my heart leave.

Bird Hands

Hollowed, glass bones
used to hold cigarettes
in Europe.
I hope for your life,
you [always] remember mine.

Finally

my stupid silly, pale white,
corrupt, gold,
scratched, tattooed knuckles
have something to say,
something besides poetry.

they are my mouth,
hammers putting words down,
like graffiti ornaments,
prison sentences longer than days and days
and days and days and days and days and so on and so forth.

my mom used to say she supposed.

I wonder what my mom would say
if she saw me now...
Would she be sober?
Would she be proud?

Couldn't Sleep

Through all the eats
and the facts
and the rain
and the photographers,
and I...

I will be hers...
and hungry at midnight,
yet never never ever yawning.

PunchFuck

Daughters will say
they see water.
Sons will say
they see land.

By time and stag horns,
we all scream out the day
and we all die.
PunchFuck my heart
back to life.

Laugh at the stay-away.
Count your shotglasses.
Be afraid.
And Play.

To a happy haunted house.
To an upside down hill.
L'chaim!
We are overrun.

Fight until we are done.
Bridges over rivers.
Bridges in song.
Say everything, tangled.

The Else

on our way to our hotel,
we found ourselves
wishing we
lived there.

maybe a hundred years ago.

I cannot cry.
I go outside.
Winter smells so right.
Today.

 I will let you breathe.
If you breathe me.
Don't you agree?

The Beautiful Space Between Your Upper and Lower Eye Lids

The white and the brown.
And the blue and the teeth.
We call lashes teeth.
And I am cold.
But so hot.

Canadian Prairies

it smells different
in this wheat-fed corner of the world.
I licked the trees.

We left the city and went north,
then west,
into the winter.
We felt youthful and proud.

For all this,
we dance
during our picnic.

The wine wasn't bad,
and I am sure
the world stopped spinning for a moment.

I felt it stop
just for us, in this place of arts,
where it doesn't get any better.

You Can Trust in This

I set sail
for tomorrow
in a sail boat
made out of today and an old train.

I am not even old.
I thought I was,
but I was wrong.
I am not.

You can trust in your youth,
especially the parts of you
that I name warlocks.

A Spoonful

we put our big beers, unfinished,
on the windowsill, letting the cold alley air keep them cool for us.
when we opened our eyelid gifts, the boulevard was eating the sun.
our hearts humped, we have had a hard life this year and last.
night made us hungry, so we ate, in a brick-and-mortar store.
she had a salad, I had a sandwich, we shared a soup.
we were then carried by the words we learned.
towards the old town, down to the river.
we spat in it and watched the moon smile.
I asked her if she loved me, and she said "A spoonful..."
Then she kissed me.

Small Mansion

from under the sheets,
and into the hall.
down stone steps,
with tattooed keys.

let's meet in Virginia,
or not.
just come here,
but bring a coat.

the off-color nuanced night
begs to be in doors,
in hotel bed,
wasting fingers and letters and words.

the small love mansion
on the corner of Rue Sherbrooke and forever,
says things to libraries,
things we don't understand.

but we feel them,
urging us to get up
from under sheets
and walk into the world wearing just a robe.

The Garden Forever

not given the tools,
but I am forever the gardener.
I make stained glass windows
on weekends,
when I am not listening to the radio
or falling in love with blue eyes.

we have radishes and cherry tomatoes,
and marigolds and
and there is a turtle living in the shed
and he is friends with a prairie dog
from where they came,
I have no idea.

Surprise the mornings
with bouquets for her bed
and her heart.
She sneezes adorably.

I have a rocking chair.

Through the Dark

 we fight like artists,
drunk on porches,
using words
we used
when we were small
at times.

the neighbors
probably hate us,
but fuck them.
no one will write books
about the quiet couple
across the hall.

while god, or God,
is off somewhere singing
his own praises,
we are here on her earth,
trying our best
at living.

even if we are scared stiff
or loud and violent,
or justified or just nice,
we still acknowledge the beginnings
and the ends.
in our own little ways.

The Robin Bird and The Coyote Bastard

both
sing of the grass,
and the morning,
sign language of the wind
on backs of beasts,
begging for love
for furniture hearts
that will be burned in old chimneys
for warmth
when we are cold
and lonely.
eat of the joy,
both affection and affliction.
take life back
one day.
now watch the
morning
and try to mirror
its beware.
gallop in the rain
towards
the fear of fun.

Which Song Shall I Give You?

Should I give you a Devendra song
that I have already given to you?
Should I give you a King Khan track
that has been only mine since way back?

Should I give you a middle name?
Should I give you a city or a fool?
I just work long hours,
and chase ghosts.

Brave Not

eggs.
in your house made of doors.
the river is by us.
we are not by the river.

Hurry home to mother and figure out the doors and the killers and
the disbeliefs.
And breakfast for dinner.

Motorcycle Accident

I know I will.
There's one or two
in all of us.

Arm skin.
This is what November
tastes like?

Dreams are lost among the trees.
Sonnets are melting somewhere.
I wait to die in the shadows of words.
Somewhere stoked and wondering.

Glass marbles.
And me.
Sliding along the tasty concrete.
Just watch.

The Home

a sense of tipsy compassion,
I need you now.
by Montreal libraries,
and life,
I pray it is not all pretend.

the ground is littered with apostrophes
and sometimes songs end,
but we bend
in the wind
of what we want.

fuck and forget what we need.
as the slow violin tells me about travel,
and the sun will shine
and the moon will rise.

Every Day for the Rest of Your Life

Microwave my bones
and forget tomorrow.

Because the word *Because*
fits and fights for today
while lovers sit in parks
and daydream.

Come visit me upstairs
in the hum.

What are you in front of?

My chest cracks
as loud as loud may get.

Make Me Smile

the sight of your eyes
makes me see different things differently.

while in wild yesterland,
we stop
and go upstairs
and let ourselves laugh.

I like knowing you.

Two Forks

from the mysterious kitchen
into the heart of the violin,
I beg to differentiate myself
from the time piece
on the compassionate side of the nightstand.

while I have you as a friend,
I beg and beat the ground
into squealing alarm clocks,
and I pick myself up
off the ground.

I pray for the cheese
and the day,
and the poems
while often silly,
with stupid titles,
still sing true
to the likes of you
on hills.

.

Last Lost

I wore your necklace,
and wrote this poem on a paper bag.
Your gate and movie
will make you famous,
and twelve steps later,
through tall green grass,
you will like me as much as a backyard.

for a long time,
we wished
for more time
and more wishes
and more feet,
for the earth's beaches.

Go so far.
Publish a thirsty boy.

Hey LAW

joy is joy
and if you chose to run,
just be faithful, little bird.

you can't depend on anything
 but eyes...
and loyalty.

Pancakes

of suede and sugar,
won't you dance the way you dance
and ice skate for me?
I am addicted to your unfortunate laughter.

I just poked myself
in my owned eye
with my bandana
that usually resides in my back left pocket.

then I crossed my heart and hoped to die.
there are pictures on the wall,
and everything I do reminds me of you.
spell your name, cast me backwards, listen to the loud werds that I
write.

great legs,
you make me want to be a lifeguard.
you make me want to build a playground
and then burn it down.

enjoy the crocheting
because life and love never take holidays.
I am the saltwater gypsy,
and life is for living.

in a city of lately rain,
not all of us are wanted,
yet with some weird and wayward divination,
some of us are lucky enough to speak of revolution.

Up Late Writing Sweet Dreams

Today is in the ground
and
it disappeared noisily
while
wishing over drawbridges.

Thinner days
carry the part-of-me
melodies
that carry you
and
I still see your eyes
as an autoharp.

Listening to the City's Beautiful Noise on a Wonderful Wednesday

this is the fabric to which I keep my memories sewn.
a gone vertical muse called a carousel of progress.
I was on an alligator, you were on a peacock.
hello my new, old heart
full of attack.

Writing Short Poems

for the sake of the fire in the sky,
and the gunners,
words and eyes are forever, indeed.

I know I am not the man you desired.

allow us to scuffle on paper,
stubborn with the pen,
I believe
we can make a museum here.

Pet Project (In Said Kitchen)

kitty litter sticks to my bare feet.
at table.
in kitchen.
in two-bedroom flat.
in Outremont.
better than Brooklyn.
there is a box leaning on the wall.
the cat is brown.
the beautiful bird, bagged, is still sleeping.
and I, without knowing it, just drank expired milk.
in said sad kitchen.
barely any natural light.
especially after a horribly wonderful winter night.
boozed-up on bicycles.
bequeathing up.
out of bounds.
we met in the Plateau.
made our way downtown.
made our way to bedrooms.
now silent in said kitchen.
considering a fever.
considering disappearing.
hoping she'll think on me with more than just a laugh.
the cat comes back.
the roommate must've made coffee before she left for work.

Story Birds

dear Story Birds,
will you come visit us
up below?

fish eat our feet here.
my heart is still inside my chest.

don't leave me here with sheriff.

it's time to fly north
instead of south.

you will miss the humming of the scientific spring,
but you will get biscuits
every morning.

it's been so long,
since I've given you away.
I built a silo.

you can perch on it
and see forever
and sing.

Sad Poem

the courage
lies mistakenly
in blankets,
protected by three Elizabeths.

Pictures of Stairs

Luckily October lasted all year.
And all year was trickery.
April was okay.
Because of the books.
September 21st was supposed to be better.
I have Pictures of stairs to prove it.
With thirty-something peaches.
Scattered all over the stoop steps.
We threw all our dreams into bed.
We ate water.
I woke up a year later.

Hardy Fucking Har Har!

let's not fuck around
inside afternoons
only to kill buildings
by time and existentialism.

let's get good.
quick.

Caribou Coffee and Scotch Sour Films

I've been having trouble with doorknobs today.
Are you on top of said empire?
This is Civil War medicine.
Gift ideas for sisters: guns, knives, a canoe, a falcon.
I may very well be the invalid flood.

The day was warmish yet snow scattered.
Too much to take in, too much to hit with fists.
I sat still and gaped, wondered about history and trees.
I contemplated durability and patience.
As I stood up into the sky, I never wash my pants.

The breeze comes magnificent and serene.
I do not sway, I thought about memories.
The magazines, ripped, have seen time.
Not merely the latest.
I am the head squire in Kerouac's quest for redemption.

Even Though

I only capitalize words
when I want them
to be special,
and feel special...

and these words
do not feel special.

But today does.
Scared stiff
with iron and ring fangs,
and parking tickets.

Oh, I See Land!

after a year like this
and the one before,
I could use a stiff drink
and a kiss.

Lonely Follow

Fool-hearted fate was schooling
for the thirty-year-old children.

Like the last two or few,
following the lonely nights we call days,
this was long and a little too warm.

I can't keep waiting.
I can't keep writing this shit.

I will find my way back
to your red front door.

I need a miracle in my veins.

Poem

you are a good song.
with good lyrics.

be one of my favorites.
be the river that the townheart needs.

something is wrong.
with werds well into the beach.

I am needed so far.
stretched, the first to fall.

cut off my arms.
instead of gardening decisions.

meet me in the armless west.
we will experience new soups and revolutions.

let me give you these scars called songs.
there is no need for suspicion.

it's in eyes, not in stately violas.
it's not like knives, bury me under dandelions.

some thing is written right.
by a bastard morning without silence where it sings.

skinny love circles around hope.
becomes a disease.

poems and jokes are better.
when spelled correctly.

Aluminum/Running/Bluebird

Grey rock, dark cinder,
heart attack blues
by talking this way
up.

I want this night to last forever.

Boil Your Waters

Hurry home.
Lets love.
Play the guitar.
And the autoharp.

It is time
To decide.

Do we boil our bones in water?
Or do we chop our hearts in half?

Just to give each other one of the halves.
Just to hold on to.
Just in case.

Coincidence

If,
While you are jogging
up and down the river,
you happen on an old black fellow
with a cane
and a beard
and some sort of old hat,
go up to him
and
tell him "Ryan Buynak cares about me."
Then just walk away.

We Bought a Scissor

Hide here.
From the snow.
Québécois bodega.
Poutine next door.
Sainte Mathieu.
Guy-Concordia.

Ruffles.
Best potato chips ever.
Couple big cans of strong LaBatt's.
Water.
Dark Chocolate Kit Kats.
Scissors!

Today is thankful.
For the snow.
And I am thankful for today.
And the way she says *Scissor*.
without the S.

Birds Are Blue

My love, you have
my favorite teeth.

McGill, oh how I would love to live in you.
You can't talk without tongue.

My snail, you have
my favorite slug.

Winter will always be ours.
My hair is short.

Parc de Turin

I slept with a soda
and waited for the Amtrak train from NYC
to roll in;
been a black-eye day.

The backseat
with feet.

It's an Oldsmobile,
an easy ugly equipage,
bought down in New fuckin' Jersey
for a hundred and forty bucks, a bag of weed, and breakfast
from the same sonofabitch that
I am picking up
at the moment.

Part of me still believes
the car is hot.
He stole it,
and gave it to me when I told him
that I was escaping to Montreal
for a month or two.

Vernon is a wandered like me
and wandered into my world
after a girl and a hurricane,
both Sandras.

He wanted mountains and merriment;
I gave Parc Turin and a flannel
shirt to throw up on.

His first night in Montreal
we got drunk at Les Foufounes Électriques.
We walked home through Parc Turin,
ugly wind, bought drugs,
and wondered what November would bring.

I Have Sixteen Hundred Tigers

 reinvent your name.
I never meant to say these words:
a thousand ways to try.

tinkering, poetic.
there is smoke in the sky.
I am catching a train
and that train is heading to you.

we weird hearts
from the tumbling start.
can you still not remember who is hiding up there?

one day as a bicycle.
one day as a lion.
one day as a winter river yet.
one day as a bottle of ketchup with a little mayonnaise in it.

meet me in the fields after a morning of desire.

there is no real goodbye if you mean it.

Jukin'

we were with montrealistik
in the freshpaintgallery.

and then...

and then *Buskwick Blues* by Delta Spirit comes on.
and then *St. Joseph's* by The Avett Brothers comes on.
and then *Home* by Edward Sharpe comes on.
and then *Skinny Love* by Bon Iver comes on.

A Typical Side Street in Verdun

I'm on so-and-so street
and the morning fog is so thick
that I can't even see Bannantyne Street,
the next block over.

I finally see the headlights of the bus.
sometimes I pay the fare,
sometimes I don't.
the drivers who make barely enough to survive
could care less.

exhaust fills the air,
and now my fears come to me
two by two,
slapping my side when I transfer
at so-and-so street.
Someday I won't waste anymore time.

Notre dame de grace!
Gotta work.
I've texted her from this bathroom
before,
in great gone force.

It took too long
for the day to die.
Greatness is bestowed upon me,
and this is where
I do the dishes.

The red is mine
just like the brown.
Stars are certainly here.
Something makes them shine
when I hug her over brunch.

By night, before beer work I strut.

The first hours of the evening
of what is left in this part of Montreal.

All our happy behaviors
deliver me
to dangerous
bells and cassettes.

There's always
another girl
and another
day.

Talk About

There's too much blood in my body
so I accidentally let some out
via my ring finger.

I Have Important News!

Crawl.
The sky sweats rain.
I like that we died today.
Twice.

A Postcard of Apricots in Four Lines

I shoot at peaches.
I like cobwebs.
I was born for your kiss.
And the never-ending rain.

Oscar Put Down the Knife

We can start our own town
outside of existentialism.

Good.
I think you should.
Somewhere near the Desmond sidewalk.

We wait
for weekends.

Please don't ruin my life.

I have nothing else to say
to ants or ears.

Good shine.
Peacocks and cola
in the trees.
Municipal court tomorrow
and fire tonight.

I Know Something You Don't Know

Life is fine.
Come hither
and show yourself sure.

Walked Up 40 Hills

I hope it is me
you write about.

Yeh!
My paper bag in a heart.

We get weird near
Lachine Canal,
and get sick
into it.

Last night was lovely
and loud
and long,
lasting into today's funny papers.

You could turn me over
just with your eyes
in half that time.

Your Only Souvenir is a Suitcase Full of Sand
(for Tokyo Police Club)

when we were compromised
in that Brooklyn bastard summer
that sucked the wind out of the trees
and our open skies,
we wished in silence
and sang on trampolines,
while spirits were slender
and we were just trying to let ourselves off the hook.

I knew your blue eyes better than anything.

And the radio knew just what to play.

Lamps and Boats

I get lost and I find things.
I get my selfishness from my mother.

Save our eyes for snacks.
We are a miracle in color.

Fuck.
My heart hurts.

I wait for you.
Indoors.

I want to build a house.
And fill it full of lamps.

I want to buy a boat.
And sink it.

Poem

The way you were
when you were on my shoulders.
Singing woe.
Gone and being.

The Future Is Ours

I remember the train.
Now.
Not.
Before.

These outerlines
that bring me here every year,
like searching...
I've won four out of five.

This is the epidermis.
of songs
that you can use
to send envelopes
to way-back-when.

Brains

Manicures
and
pedicures
before
we leave.

I am the lump sum
of cowboys
and pirates
and symptoms
and folk heroes.

I will stay
the same.

We talk
while we walk
past big bronze hearts,
past libraries
with brains in them.

We don't have brains.
We only have hearts
with secrets and pioneers.

Victory

For posterity and self-defense,
I do not wear pants while I write.
Not tonight, at least,
not here in my Montreal.

The shape we are in
at the bottom of this mountain,
will change the shape
of our wayward untimely climbing lives.

I wish I were a ghost
with teeth
forever,
under a white table cloth
with two holes poked in the top.

From Snowdon to Saint-Michel

It is just like the motherfucking future
to be showing up like this.

With a bang,
we start to kiss.

And I say on the metro
that I don't want to fall in love.

Excited

I am so excited for the next book...
For the next season...
For the next rain.

it is so great and weird and on fire...
from the desert...
that I don't need anymore.

From Montmorency to Cote-Vertu

I know this well.
This blast.
This line.

Only love is on the move.
Blooming flowers.
The sky is wounded.
She is the scythe moon.

I am not my mother.
On the wall.
Moving waters.
So we are sure.
I want to fall deep deep deep into love.
Like a well.

Hunting Cap

It is old
and red
with a shearling inner lining,
and it is a little too snug,
and the shearling has,
over the years,
turned grey.

Like me,
it is ugly,
but it is lucky,
especially in the awesome autumn,
and it sure is warm.

I bought it in a thrift shop
four or five years ago
in Mile End,
and never washed it once.

God only knows how old it is.

Poem

It feels like folk music.
playing hard into closing hospital.

My mind is a creative professional.

I see the sadness
of the Seder.

Polka dots
are the fire in some sort of frost.

Festivals were never buffalos.

The Photographs

Perfect graves
for the time of tidbits
and while
the whole world
blinks by
these photographs will always be mine.

Even if I scowl
and blue birds bend the background,
we will find the voice
and gears
of the wind
while it riddles through your famous eyes.

Spreading the Windows Apart

Take me from this medicine
and this mountain.
I will get rid of all our love
from that know-it-all horizon.

Hell, I am still standing on this corner
where I left you.

I've set the sun to be bright
to wake my wife up.

Your Boring Road

I pull on my boxer briefs,
as they grow in peace,
in the Chateau Versailles.

I believe
I kill sounds
behind me.

Your boring road
is my beautiful back alley,
and I don't give a fuck
about anything else
anymore.

Fuck The Summer

My life hates the summer sky.
And the reasons why.
Shake the bed.
With a thunder strike.
From my hand.
We lay in sheets.
With tomahawks.
And a lion's mouth.

Scarecrow Trees

I remember my mother.
Her name was William.
She sang like Vernon.

I didn't give her much of a sun.
I gave rain.
But she gave me absolutely nothing.
Maybe some sort of tiny tiny dense creative shit genes.

But I am in.
This world.

I know.
This is.
The best.
Breath.
To take.

Let's Learn to Throw Knives

the weather sucks here in
Le Plateau.
I take that back,
the rain is rather romantic
to us poets.

I want to be your favorite color,
because, to me,
you look like a reason to live.

The muffin man lives
on the very top of Mont-Royal
with the outlaws and us,
lovers,
and
while we figure out the ditch sitch,
I love the way Canadian whiskey makes my
body feel,
and
I love the way your heart
makes my
heart feel.

Find a Little Thing

Look at my roof!
I take piss off it.
And it shouldn't be a roof at all.

This roof is blue.
Elm Street.
This is Montreal.
Like Matt Pond said so eloquently.

We are.
West of Downtown.
Reading Romeo and Juliet.
All over again.
Aloud.
At night.
And dying to relearn the end.

We are.
Eighteen insulation.
Well, now I've seen everything.
Love and lightning.
Twice.
Wait till the wind whips up.

Even in a painting,
a thunderstorm
is perfect.

Those Windows

Those two iconic windows
behind our window point-of-view
stand as a symbol of silent years of lovely escape.

They are what we saw each morning
when I would open the curtains
and drink last evening's beer.

Hell, they even grace the cover of this book.

That's right,
this book is self-aware.
maybe too self-aware.

Like me.

Sweeter Than the Moon

Shy-Shy's face was priceless.
Kayle was tired, but happy.
Franco arrived later.
Franco is like an ape or a toddler,
except he is more like a cat.
But my friends are all sweeter than the moon.

Out of the Woods

life is hard,
but fun,
and sometimes
so very beautiful,
and honestly,
dear insulted audience,
I think I have begun
to figure things out;
things I didn't
or couldn't understand
or comprehend
at any younger age.

Thank you.

Coffee and Kisses Tomorrow

I ask a question
and the answer is breakfast.

While salads burn bright by day
in afternoon has-beens,
and we are here for chocolate.

Choose a bagel at St. Viateur.

This today is tomorrow.
And I eat it.
As girls.

Eat.
You.
Sweet.

Through the Broken Bones of the Better of My Soul

I killed June and July
just for you,
and wished for October and September,
the 21st and the 26th
respectively,
and nobody said
anything about love and death in November.

Reviewed

It started raining.
Bite to eat?
Au Pied du Cochon.
I stink.
And the hostess was a nasty bitch.
Bar.
Beer.
foie gras.

Forgetting this will forever be impossible.
That's how badly great it was.
It adds up, like mad math, to something Yelp can never review.

Cambria Bold

the simon red
of the skid...
even in the skid,
I find an archaic playground swing.
Point St. Charles.
Even.

this is the way I believe in.
this is my hunger.
My muse.
This is my sentence.

Who knows?
Who knows?
Who knows
for sure.

I wait.
For make-up.
For her.
I said rejoice.

I loved her more than I loved myself.

Editing In A Montreal Hotel Room

if I had my way,
this shit would start with ellipses.
my old gossipy friends bark like a unison dog,
doesn't mean they don't deserve good grammar.
I'm a darn good driver.
Easy equipage.
Let's kill this shit.
The dead pig came around
saying that particular exclamation point has gotta go.
it went away from that sentence,
along with spinster gin that let's nobody in.
not a grumpy island,
but I have never felt before that the semi-colon
would make me want to cry.
it did.
I mapped this drunk,
then brainstormed sober.
business as usual for a wordsmith.
get busy living like syllables.
everybody's wishing for no more mistakes,
and all that I can think about is you.
let's go be great.
period.

Poem

Forever the fuckin' olive branch!
I was gonna start at sickness.
Art goes to sleep.
I knew when I was about to write.
Especially about love or loss or love again.
I will give you these songs
if you listen to them loud.

Folk Hero

we pour songs
and draw knives...
this is my last song about myself.

no regrets
and I will not ask for your forgiveness.
sail away, it will all make sense.
we can still be good
without righteousness.

if you are full of faith,
then you are faithful...
timing is everthing.

new wolf teeth,
new forest,
only love,
the innocent collection.

Sylvia and Geppetto

We are not old at all.
Just too old for fucking around.

At least to measure our skulls.
Vs.
Our hearts.

Turn our shoulders to the empty space.
And start our own town.

Every writer has a cold heart.
Sylvia boils mine in brine.

Bad news always comes.
On the Yankee wire.
But it is up to us.
To pull it out with gasoline.
And set some happiness on fire.

Vieux-Montréal

I'm walking, I like the wind.

Cradles and rain and animals
hear us
while we never really break.

Whether at a Sears in Deltona,
or in an apartment over
a grandma's home
in Long Island,
or in a cobble stone alley in Vieux-Montréal,
we live with our decisions
and lose our breath to beauty.

With Generosity and a Quicksilver Tongue

Today was your last
night,
wasn't it?

www.ingramcontent.com/pod-product-compliance
Lightning Source LLC
Chambersburg PA
CBHW060805050426
42449CB00008B/1551